TOPOGRAPHY OF DREAMS

Poems by
MJ Moore

BLUE LIGHT PRESS ✦ 1ST WORLD PUBLISHING

SAN FRANCISCO ✦ FAIRFIELD ✦ DELHI

Topography of Dreams

BLUE LIGHT PRESS
www.bluelightpress.com
bluelightpress@aol.com

1ST WORLD PUBLISHING
PO Box 2211
Fairfield, IA 52556
www.1stworldpublishing.com

BOOK & COVER DESIGN
Melanie Gendron
melaniegendron999@gmail.com

INTERIOR ILLUSTRATION
Melanie Gendron

COVER PHOTO
Robert L. Creighton

AUTHOR PHOTO
David L. Creighton

FIRST EDITION

Library of Congress Cataloging-in-Publication Data

ISBN: 978-1-4218-3684-3

For David and Robbie

Acknowledgements

I want to thank the following journals and anthologies, which have published several of these poems, in some cases revised: *riverbabble, Bach in the Afternoon* (Blue Light Press), *Museum Collection* (Didcot Writers), *Nightingale and Sparrow, The Avocet, The Sky Away from Here* (Blue Light Press), and *Vistas and Byways*.

Poetry may seem like a solitary art, but in my experience it is communal, and its devotees are among the wisest and most joyful people in the world. I would like to thank the writing groups that have welcomed me over the last three years for their encouragement, suggestions, and multiple viewpoints. A special thank you goes to Heather Estes, who led the way with her own book, and who offered her advice, wisdom and humor at the outset of my book. I offer my heartfelt gratitude to Diane Frank, a wonderful writer and teacher, whose workshops inspired me to return to poetry, hone my skills, delve into my heart, and write. Her vision and guidance have been invaluable.

To my son Robbie and my husband David, I have appreciated your enthusiasm and comments on my poems and your many readings and discussions about matters big and small. Above all, thank you for your belief in me and your love.

Table of Contents

Topography of Dreams

Kaleidoscopic World

I

Fire-Burst Seed

Journey

The first step is always a miracle.
The splash of paint on the palette,
a vigorous swirl,
and two colors collide.
Perhaps a pigment
that reverberates through time,
centuries back,
and breaks the heart.
Perhaps a new hue —
disturbing citron, breathtaking sapphire.
A color that people will nod and say,
Van Gogh yellow, Monet blue.
Brush strokes that speak their own language,
sing down the nerve endings,
and propel our fingers to trace the air.

Maybe it begins with a mélange of words,
a marvelous phrase that wakes you up at night,
drums in the brain
until it spills out, a wild bloom.

You never know where you're going.
Could be across the ocean.
Could be straight over the hill
and down to the white cottage.
The journey may take a perilous turn,
into dense trees that thicken
in a tyranny of branches and roots,
closing to an unsure end.

Here is the ageless heart of the mystery.
The white-clad maiden, barefoot,
relinquishes armor, weapons, guile,
and steps into the dark,
knowing this is her calling,
this is her path.

Wedding Day

On our wedding day, the minister, a friend,
spoke about Arctic expeditions,
Franklin's failure.
How ice trapped his ship,
and the men dragged silverware on sleds for miles
before collapsing from the weight.
How they ignored the Inuit hunters,
who could have counseled them
on how to stay alive.

Strange words for a festive day — yet prescient.
Who needs advice for balmy days?
Like all who attempt this journey,
we have trod polar ice through blinding storms,
compass shattered by howling winds.
We have lost each other in white-outs,
drifted for days in darkness.

We jettisoned the silver,
trained ourselves to live lean, cut losses,
cinch the belt tighter.
We learned when to listen
to wind's merest whisper,
when to drive the team or let it rest,
how to cut out festering flesh,
wrap the wound firmly,
trudge on.

Along the journey, a world worth living —
crystal stars in obsidian sky.
Curtains of color arc overhead,
and cold clear air sparks the soul.

Scorched

On a scorched Miami night,
a girl's hot bare feet creep up pale cool walls,
tracing the old smudged path.
A pearl of sweat blossoms and spills on the bed.
An opera tenor blares from the warped hi-fi,
a heart-breaking *miserere* —
"Lord, have mercy on my soul."

One a.m.

Outside, moths batter themselves
against the fizzing porch light,
circling their moon.

On nights like this
her mind stumbles through the garden maze,
seeking the torched center, longing
for the way out.

When the World

When the world comes crashing down,
all the streamers and bright-colored balls,
the artificial, airy structures
constructed with blithe and perfect faith
burst and plummet.
Hold the tattered shreds and empty husks,
holy as first light and final star.

You cannot build again.
No retracing, no rewinding,
no perfect ending
waiting in the highest branches.
Only the threads of raucous crows —
prophets adamant and shrill.

Rags draped over your outstretched arms,
palms up, you have only this to proffer —
a benediction of ruin,
held luminous as a feather,
now resting,
now spinning away,
the softest breath of life.

Full Garden

White curtains shimmer in the breeze
above her hospice bed.
In response to my grief,
she says, Construct a garden.
Plant every flower you've ever coveted.
Don't worry about a plan.
A pretty pattern is not the purpose here
but a deeper beauty, wild and chaotic,
like truth or hope.

Fill your garden with roses and peonies,
lilies and irises.
You can concentrate color
or vary height and hue.
Create movement, ripple and flow.
Plant thick and fast
so that your hands find no time for regret.

Flowers need homes —
your heart or somewhere else.

And why not yours?
I've seen how it follows sun's heat,
unfolds to bees, soaks in the smell of dirt and rain.
Celebrates seasons' flow.

Take these seeds, scratch a furrow,
cover them with loam.
I promise to be here next year
in all my bright, leafy glory.

Dark Enchantment

I met him once —
that great Irish poet,
on a camping trip on Carrauntoohil.
He appeared beyond a boulder,
then hiked with us for miles
over stony slopes, under gray-shrouded skies.
Mist rose from the gorse,
curled around scuffed boots,
as his sonorous voice recounted ancient tales.

He was free with the girls —
his hands heavy around their shoulders,
depthless blue eyes piercing their untried souls.
I didn't really like him —
the way he just reached out and took,
thinking he had a right
to whatever bright thing he wanted,
although many were willing enough.

I was chilled by his power —
and maybe a bit jealous.
He wove his spell, then disappeared,
leaving an indelible mark.

Imprint

"I have slept with my cheek against the earth."
— Erin Rodoni

I have slept in the forest of my dreams,
cheek pressed against the earth
like a lover or child.
My skin has borne the primal mark of leaves,
and my memory, the dark smell of mushrooms sprouting.

I have heard small creatures scramble
through tree roots,
watched ants stagger under enormous burdens.

I have tasted water flashing off rocks
and chased it down the riverbed.
Shivering in green air at dusk,
I have inhaled the nighttime promise
of death, transmutation, rebirth.

In the unexpected moments —
when we stoop to hoist the laundry
or stand shuffling in the grocery line —
the places we leave the imprint of our bodies
remember us, send a message:

Come back to this haven,
where joy is carved in the heart
and desire is home.

Art and Algebra

Framed in gilded curlicues, Arabian maidens
trail slender fingers in a pool,
green with sun and age.
Aristocratic boy in faded blue,
eyes brimming with disdain, hand stuffed
in waistcoat like a budding Napoleon,
looks down his nose.
Androgynous child, auburn curls arrayed
over lace frills,
cuddles an oddly stoic rabbit.

Beneath this outmoded art,
orange clashes with green
in the sofa's bursting floral print.
Chewed coffee rugs lap zones
of tropical terrazzo.
Brown kitchen cabinets and aqua Formica
confront the crowded dining room
and bruised Hammond organ.

I teethed on a riot of mismatch,
a festival of shabby.
Mom was not an interior decorator.

My friends' homes whispered
of elegance, monochromatic tranquility.
Their mothers choreographed movement
through a room, taught their daughters
how to place an object just so,
to make the eye glide and then rest.

Mom instead embraced the calm beauty
of precise equations, refined proofs.
Math was her dance;
teaching, her true love.
She waltzed students, myself included,
through the intricate steps
of algebra's heady dip and twirl.
With her, we claimed the mastery of our minds.

Magic Stone

Night is the magic stone.
Rub it and sparks fly.

I'm seven or eight, head on Mom's lap, eyes closed.
Words swirl overhead,
waver and bend like Northern Lights,
the meanings luminous, shifting.
They think I am asleep, but I am listening,
    always listening,
absorbing sounds as they talk into the dark.

Tucked against her stomach,
I feel words echo,
reverberate to our matched pulse.
Arms wave, hands clap to smoky incantations.
Feet drum to the ancient dance.
Fantastic flames whirl high into black sky,
snatch at stars,
fall back, again, again, again,
until molten, they flow,
a stream,
    a river,
        a torrent rushing
            towards the deep and silent sea.

Vivace

for Carol

Deaf in one ear, you always sat on my left,
gossiping about Faure's affairs,
praising Schumann's concertos,
as we waited in the silence between sounds.

You taught me how to listen
as the instruments create a universe.
The violins flaunt a phrase,
share it back and forth,
then the cellos commandeer the motif
and weave a counterpoint.
French horns scoop up the notes,
bend and brighten them,
while percussion marks time
till the final crescendo.

You gripped my arm
to signal transcendent parts.
We leaned into melancholy,
held our breaths for menace,
in harmony, released.

With you almost blind now, confined
in a room too small for your spirit,
we talk by phone. In the background,
Beethoven, Tchaikovsky or Mahler
swells and subsides.
Long after we hang up,
the final notes vibrate and ache.

House of Redwood

This house is built of redwood,
ancient and wise
as fire-burst seed and ocean salt.

On clear nights, I sit at the window
and scan the eastern hills,
spangled with street and porch light
and the firefly drift of cars.

But on windy, rainy nights,
as branches whip the light-lost home,
flash and rattle insist a different memory,
millennia old.

Incantations of bird and bug wing,
the soft slither of night creatures
along the damp forest floor.
Pungent decay permeates
the liquid twilight,
layers of sentience compressed,
a vow of death and birth.

Bitter thorn and sweet fern
tumble in cyclic thrall of primacy and passion.
Muddy torrents rip branches, trunks, roots,
and hurtle over the precipice.

I have marked my son's years
against the doorpost,
mistaking solid walls for acquiescence.

My heart bows in this brief instant
to time's flood.
All honor and praise,
heartwood and pith.

Ballooning

Last evening in wavering light,
you shared your journey back
through ancestral homes and youthful dreams.
A litany of love and loss
and losses to come.

All night I dreamed of ballooning.
Hundreds of spiderlings
flinging up gossamer strands and clinging
as the wind tossed them further and further away.
I felt their weightlessness and abandon,
the restless urge that drove them miles from home.

No thought for what's left behind,
the moments they will not share.
They loose their moorings and, carefree,
set themselves adrift.

II

Lapis

Lapis

I have never loved diamonds —
incorruptible, transparent,
flawless except to a jeweler's loupe.
Hard enough to drill down
and demolish the heart's dark core.

Nor am I a pearl,
hung lightly around
a chaste, alabaster neck.
White, luminescent,
radiating peaceful perfection.

I am lapis lazuli,
semi-precious stone
dug from soaring crags
of the Hindu Kush.

A crystalline amalgam
of meandering minerals,
veined like an ancient hand
sculpting ageless rites.

Rock crushed, heated,
morphed in earth's cauldron
into brilliant shades of blue,
spattered with dross,
shot through with fire.

Hands

"I have seen them when there was nothing else."
— *W.S. Merwin, "The Hands"*

At first light my hands
slap warmth into cold cheeks.
At bedfall they extinguish the light.
Have they ever known a still moment?

They slather with soap,
scour mud-splattered walls,
forever scrubbing the persistent grime
that smothers every surface.

Scrabbling at deeply embedded rocks,
careless, slashed by thorns,
my broken hands
battle stubborn clay.

Even in sleep they grasp the blanket
that slips from my restless shoulders.
Always busy, they defy wisdom,
too proud for peace.

Never matched in prayer,
they scorn supplication or succor.
Why not let them cradle each other —
or another?

Flying Squirrel

Last week in the garage, I found it buried in a box.
Slightly mildewed, one eye gone, leaking sawdust —
my stuffed toy squirrel,
with its equivocal smile.
A Christmas present from my aunt.

How I loved that squirrel!

Laughing, I flung it out the bedroom window
to my brother, waiting in the alley
two stories below.

He crouched, leaped, and clawed.
When it hit the gravel,
a shower of pebbles sprayed out.
He grabbed it and flung it back.
We terrorized that squirrel for hours, day after day.
Still it survived.

Why have I kept it all these years?
Not sentimentality.
Rather, fierce loyalty to a thing that,
without resentment,
would bear such battering.

Trophy

As a child, I dug up sand dollars
with my bare toes, relishing the cool squish
of mud against pale skin.
A small accomplishment of dexterity.

My fingers brushed the rough hairs,
held alien life as it faded.
Each day I checked as the sun
bleached them to brittle white.

Childhood trophies on a faded shelf.
I caress the smooth skeletons,
shake free grains of sand
still hidden at the core,
and recall the pleasures
of a heedless heart.

Four Rings

The tiny ruby shone on my finger.
A gift when I was 8, the same age
as when your mother gave it to you.
You beamed at my joy.
So few heirlooms survived
when your home burned in your teens.

One night, unseen,
it slipped from the bathtub rim.
I sobbed to sleep while you patted my back.
Next morning, somber, I said, "No more rings."

Old enough to love,
too young for stewardship.
For years we kept the pact.

At graduation, I knew what I wanted.
A star sapphire,
milky white ablaze in azure,
set in silver swirl.
It hugged my finger till my wedding day.

After your funeral, the envelope held two rings.
One a gold band worn through,
one an empty setting
where a diamond once gleamed.

Plundered

We all know what it means.
The phone ringing at 5:00 a.m.,
the vibrating rope that yanks you
from wet, green depths
to heart-panting light,
the groping wish for a wrong number,
the familiar name trumpeted on the display.

My brother cries softly,
"Mom died last night."
"But I wanted to see her one last time."
"I know you did."

As the dream world descends,
the will rises, ghost-like, assumes command.
Flight plans, breakfast, flowers, calls to friends.
The formal line of tasks.

We know how to adult,
to talk in measured words,
pack the dark dress,
present a red yet calm face.

But in the burned, gutted shell of the soul,
tiny legs and arms flail,
and infant voice, desperate, screams,
"Mine, mine, mine!"

Grainy Film

Remarkably, my brother's lined and veined hands
recall how to thread the dusty 8 mm reels.
We have waited 20 years to confront
this clutter of childhood memories.

Dim, fuzzy images speed past —
driving through dappled redwoods,
throwing snowballs in summer mountains,
plunking blueberries into a stained baseball cap.

Early family expeditions
when Dad was still the hero
who hung the moon and stars.

"I remember that!"
"Yes, I do, too."
We reclaim bonds from untarnished times,
before the garden gate slammed shut.

In the last reel, at Yellowstone,
we pose at the edge of simmering sulfur pools
in miraculous turquoise and maroon.
We see the steam and huge bubbles,
remember the menacing smell and heat.
The same prickly fear as Dad urges us
to step back, closer to the brink.

How We Leave

Unsteady State

Sun sparks off fluttering black wings.
Starlings in formation twist,
vanish into light.

Wind bustles into the plaza.
White petals eddy,
swirl between feet, then depart.

Slow Fade

Hands stuffed in pockets,
she frowns, turns,
dissolves into night.

A car door slams.
Engine hum swells and fades.

Window curtains close,
extinguish the light.

The Sea

Ocean fog billows,
obliterates sky and land.

A storm of words meant to drown.
Easier than a quiet good-bye.

Mountain Light

As we drive vertiginous mountain roads,
our bodies curve with the bends,
all engines revving.

On the ridge, midsummer rays
pierce the treetops. From vertical cliffs
pines lift up twisted boughs,
supplicants to sun.
Under dense forest canopy,
interlaced limbs quell the light.

Wide grassy strips among the trees
reveal the history of avalanche —
where in deep winter snowpack
icy bonds shattered,
and a catastrophe of weight thundered down.

We all long for what we lack —
sun in dark forest,
stability on a slippery slope,
release from an unbearable burden.

Slot Canyon

Contorted stone, a cavern
of continuous twist and surprise.
Undulating orgy of scarlet rock.

Shifting sand on canyon floor
coats jeans and skin.
Silt deadens sound
as shoes whisper like lizard feet
around the ribbon bends.

Swirl of rigid rock urges fingers
to trace the ancient sway.
Filtered light
unveils a holy labyrinth.

Returned to silent desert hills,
we are not who we were.
Red dust has replaced molecules of bone.

Like sand compelled by eons of wind,
we ripple, flow, and whirl.

Splashing in the Stream

A sangha is a Buddhist spiritual community.

On August retreat, sangha sisters
stand in a child's wading pool,
hot feet submerged in cold water.
A chattering, singing flock,
splashing joy on a parched day.

Waving the hose, I gently spray them.
As they spin and squeal,
a scene from 30 years ago bursts open.

At my son's daycare, we had debated
the risk of a homeless man
who slept in the center's empty planter.
Each day, when we reclaimed our infants,
he waved the hose like a wand,
splashing water on the churchyard roses.
His face was beatific, full
of wonder at sun's sparkle on the stream.
We decided, "He's harmless."
The roses thrived.

One day, he was gone.
My tiny son looked at the empty space,
frowned, turned to me.
I had no answer.

Today, I lift hands in gratitude
for that chance to have imagined
someone else's need,
to open my heart
and fill a beggar's bowl.

As we depart on different paths,
our own bowls in this moment filled,
I sing a new mantra:
May all hearts dance in the brilliant stream.

III

War Museum

The War Remnants Museum

Ho Chi Minh City, 2018

In the museum of death,
black-framed photos hang
on gray, pock-marked walls.
A girl runs screaming from her own skin.
Laughing sergeants sit on their haunches,
finger beads strung around their necks.
An unexpected bullet shatters
a shackled soldier's brain.

In cracked display cases, dim light
illuminates declarations, proclamations, treaties.
Designers of death shake hands.
Words bury worlds.

Outside, a bloom of metal carcasses —
helicopters, troop transports, cannons, tanks
droop in blistering sun.

Who holds the candle?
Who prays into the night?
Who watches the stars blink and cluster
across the sky?

Who scratches words in a worn notebook?
Recalls a rifle's crack.
Drowns in dark dreams
amidst waving reeds.

Hoi An

I

Colored lanterns everywhere —
dangling in shops, swaying over alleys,
floating down the river.
Reminders to live lightly,
illuminate the dark.

II

Driving a hard bargain,
I feel strangely empty.
No one smiles.

III

Bamboo poles, held side-by-side,
pound the floor, clack together —
Mua Sap, an ancient children's game.
Tipsy tourists skip between the sticks,
dodge and stumble.
Musicians trap a pale ankle or bare toe,
share smug smiles.

IV

Small wooden Buddha head,
serene among fat, beaming bronzes.
Did someone sell this
to buy a bowl of noodles?

As I sit cross-legged in my room,
the image settles in my hand.
I rub a smooth cheek
and silently chant a mantra
for past and future lives,
incense rising toward imagined heaven.

Nagaloka

*A training center in Nagpur, India, for Buddhist youth
who have been subjected to untouchability*

Arrival

On a warm noisy night,
our car rattles onto the school grounds,
escaping the clatter and roar
of diggers and trucks,
the blaring lights of a city
under constant construction.

Ahead, a 50-foot golden Buddha
steps into moonlight.

Lizards

Under an inviting sun,
lizards warm themselves on brown brick walk,
small striped bodies breathing.

As feet approach, they flee,
wriggle under drooping leaves,
await passing judgement.

Class Talk

The instructor requests an impromptu talk.
I smile and improvise.
My topic—Patience.
With the demands of others,
with procedures, queues, questions.
The self's hungry desire to disappear
into comfort and home.

Shrine

Before entering the shrine
we remove our shoes,
abandon them in a sea of sandals.
Across castes, continents, centuries,
the same dirt on the bottom of our feet.
The same smile on the Buddha's lips.

Matriarchs

Feeding time at Chiang Mai Elephant Preserve

Grandmother Elephant sways
in wide expressive arcs.
Dusty brown ears, freckled with pink,
frayed at edges like threadbare carpet,
flap and wave.
Rope tail, tipped in black bristles,
whips at her back.
From more than twice my height,
her small startled eyes stare down.

I raise the banana high, announce *"Bon."*
Obediently, she opens her mouth.
As I place my offering on her full pink tongue,
giant gums gently mash my hand.
Softly, I trace grooves and wrinkles
on leathery trunk.

Imitating her dance,
I weave back and forth in counterpoint,
intoxicated by imagined intimacy.
Just a thin bamboo fence separates us.

Later, her *mahout* says, "Elephants don't dance.
That's a sign of mental illness.
She's been mistreated."

At day's end we squeeze sideways
into the back of the open truck.
In a cloud of dust and diesel incense,
the rutted road rocks me to fitful dreams.
Malevolence smolders as forests burn.
With Grandmother Elephant, I keen and sway.

Silver Rain

In the meditation hall, I sit in silver light.
Beyond the open walls,
rain drips from the Bodhi tree,
whispers on the walk.
A candle illuminates the Buddha.

To protect against cows and monkeys,
I have shut the temple's outer gate.

A small gray lizard,
knowing its own mind,
slips across the stone floor,
rests briefly at my feet,
then runs for the shrine.

Flying into Night

Hurtling through clouds
defies the gravity of reason.
Strapped tightly in 30 cubic feet,
I inhale recycled air.
The only solution
is to hum a Broadway tune,
regardless of who stares.
Or loose the seatbelt,
slide into the aisle,
ignore the attendant's polite demand
to sit, buckle up, study the screen.

I shed my shackled carnate self
and stare from outside the window,
nose pressed against glass,
into the stuffed, hermetic world.

Twelve hours from home.
Halfway around the world
is a prophetic distance.

Outside, unyielding darkness
rushes towards us.

In the Borderlands

Lucky are those who live in enchanted realms,
with arable soil, rich in rain.
Some souls, less fortunate,
are born in Life's borderlands.
Wild, barren desert where corn crops fail
and despair tracks flagging feet.
Peace, only a mirage.

How does hope survive?
This death-hungry world teaches us
to stumble on,
breathe in deeply the searing blue sky,
learn the language of this stark land.

Silence exposes the rattle
before the snake can strike.
Heavy tread scatters the scorpions.
Black crusts of earth harbor a universe
of lichen, bacteria, moss.
Ocotillo knows the weight of water,
cradles and savors each drop.

In deep twilight, our prickly, stubborn hearts
remember the miracle of purple sage
in brief and brilliant bloom.

In Lieu of Flowers

In lieu of flowers please send . . .

A ball of twine and cookie crumbs
to retrace the path.
Compass, orienteering book,
topographic map marked with an X
to navigate this uncharted frontier.
Return, we know, is not guaranteed.

Send a silver whistle, climbing rope, wool hat.
Aspirin, a large bandage and snakebite kit.
Purification tablets for tainted water,
a packet of sugar for the bitter taste.

Don't forget the photograph
of a late-afternoon, sun-in-the-eyes smile
burned so deeply in the heart
that it will bind him to earth
forever.

Lowest Tide

Mud flats, rippled, flecked with sun,
scrabble towards the receding bay.
Streamlets reflect an unsure sky,
paddle for reed-encrusted shore.
Clouds of gulls and clapper rails skitter
over the liquid land,
peck at harried, embedded prey.

At low tide, all is laid bare,
soft underbelly exposed.

A silent prayer rises:
Come back, pulsing sea,
reclaim the pebbled shore,
sing your soft *whap whap*.
Slap against rock while splayed water
rises, twists, falls back.

Lap the edges of memory.
Retrieve a time when horizon yawned
and stretched for eons,
and heart, a nascent galaxy,
burst into radiant light.

Stirring the Soil

After the first brilliant glimpse
of the Bodhicitta —
the will to attain Enlightenment —
the slow, difficult work begins.
Stirring the soil, sifting out the worms,
gently laying them aside.
Turning over the detritus of years,
maybe eons.

You think someday, perhaps soon,
you'll strike solid rock,
the foundation, the hard "It" of the Self,
which you intend to grind to powder
and sweep away.

Meanwhile, each night as you sleep,
leaves drift down, squirrels bury acorns,
hares drop black pellets.
Rain washes in mud and fills the hole.

Each morning you rise, grasp your trowel,
doggedly remove the remains
of the previous day.

Everywhere, life reminds you of its primacy.

But one day, stiff with stooping,
you stand and stretch.
Your eyes sweep the horizon,
and your heart breathes in cedar and pine.
Long afternoon shadows
whisper in the breeze.

Rooted, you watch the sun spill over the hills,
splashing orange, red, and purple
as it disappears.
The full moon, huge yellow globe,
rises and climbs the silhouetted trees.
Pure and luminous, it pours light below
on the clear and perfect path.

IV

Topography of Dreams

Cartography

Lamplight and shadow patrol the mind's museum.
Guide and tourists drift down the corridor,
recede and vanish.

Unseen, alone, I wander an ancient atlas,
trace caravan routes, sway with camels
laden with brilliant brocade, spicy perfume.
Along the Silk Road at Samarkand,
I pause to dip my ladle in a surging spring.
Mountains stretch against scarred desert.
Cloaked in goat skin,
I trudge through snowbound passes,
hunt white fox and hare.

At the center of the hall
indigo globes slowly spin,
circled in golden stars.
Constellations of primal light.

On fading frescoes distant battles rage.
Cannon fire flashes
as ships lay siege to fortified cities.
In open water Poseidon whips
his horse to a white froth,
while all around
fantastic creatures writhe.
The topography of dreams,
charted but not traveled.

Yes, the old ones knew.
Here be dragons—
ravenous, unshackled,
and bristling with fire.

Sky Warrior

Memory picks the lock.
Returned letters from a long-sealed box
rustle at her feet.
A shiver in the warm windy night.
She sees her hand
but no longer tastes the furious fire.

Who was the girl who wrote those words?
The one who pounded on the walls of her skin,
demanded to be let out — or in?
Who shimmered on the surface
of moon-drenched lakes?
Who hunted desire with silver bow
and blood-raked arrows,
slipped barefoot and silent
among swirling stars?

Once she rode heaven's arc.
What had she dreamed?
Where did she vanish?

Penumbra

The trees are restless tonight,
not just from the quickening breeze
and whisper of rain on lake's rim.
Rooted in one place,
scored where years have carved their names,
they know something of feathered secrets.
How will-o'-wisps shimmer across the bog
while clouds obliterate the stars.
How mushroom crowns wrestle soil all night,
then burst to light for the bear's paw.
How the motherless fawn falls asleep in spring snow,
and a mouse retrieves its last seed
beneath the shadow of silent wings.

Cassandra

Fevered fear and certainty
burden her heart.

The curse of prophecy:
The seed rots before it sprouts.
Flames consume flesh before first caress.
Water tastes bitter a whole life long.

Whatever she says — ignored or twisted.

She yearns for another life,
to feel, just once, surprise.
The courage that leaps from innocence.
The thrill of a lover's unexpected touch.
The lightness of a fresh breeze
rippling over water.
The luxury of lingering on an unlined face,
imagining long, sun-filled years.

Permission to see a prism of possibility
arcing across the sky.

Desire

My body yearns to be a body of water —
to flash from stillness to roaring surf.
I want to embrace the flat expanse of a shallow shore,
heated by summer sun,
the silver constraint of a bud vase,
nourishing a single red rose.

I ache to feel the turmoil of a tumbling stream,
caressed by moss, cut by stone.
The anarchy of a wave roiled by wind,
obliterated as it thunders down.
The patience of a drainpipe puddle,
longing for the next drop.

I want to echo a gibbous moon,
reverberate from a skipped stone,
fan out from the hose
in prismatic color.
To exult as the yellow boot
leaps into muddy spray.

I hunger to be the agent of alchemy,
slowly heating in a large copper pot
full of carrots and red beans.
To celebrate in every drop
shape-shifting insight and joy.

Postcards from Night

After reading "In the Darkness" by Mary Oliver

I

Please come for a visit.
If you have trouble sleeping,
you can count stars
and listen to the planets spin.

II

Did you hear who I saw kissing
down by the dock?
Doesn't everyone know
the night has a thousand eyes?

The moon was up way past sunrise
and now she's just a pale shadow
of herself.

III

The moon is so fickle —
waxing and waning,
depending on which way she's facing.
It's been a regular thing.

But I have to admit,
when I look at Luna's shining face,
other loves are just tiny blinking dots.

Words for Enchantment

Write about love?
You may as well write about shards
of sun on wind-riffled water,
green-tinted light pulsing
in a wet redwood glen,
the smell of salt air
as the catamaran shoots over waves.
The warmth of beach sand
between circling toes,
a canopy of willows trailing damp earth.
The searing sweep of light
and foghorn blare in evening storm,
the dying chord of a heart's sonata.
The in-gasp of breath at first light,
the velvet joy of entwined skin
as night exhales.

How to Fall in Love with a City

Arrive by cab in the middle of a May Day march,
red and yellow banners whipping in the wind
as people, old and young, chant their discontent
and their dreams for justice, long-denied.

Have three tourists ask where to catch the airport bus,
as if you've been here for weeks.
Find a Thai restaurant next to your hotel
with green curry perfectly seasoned for your palate.
A cafe under blue- and white-striped awning
with fat churros to dunk in thick hot chocolate.
Ride the hotel elevator to the rooftop pool
and down to the outdoor bar,
kissing in both directions.

Wander up the boulevard and marvel
at the surprise of ancient Gothic
entwined with Art Nouveau.
Stop at the Cathedral plaza, where children
chase huge, wobbling bubbles,
splashing laughter in the afternoon sun.
Sway to guitar and sax players as they sing
in a language mysterious yet familiar.
Drop *euros* into the crumpled hat
and collect your smiling bow.

And when one morning you must leave,
filled with your secret,
whisper your love and scatter
a heartful of petals from the train window,
knowing you could dwell in this dream forever.

Extravagant Seasons

Each morning imagination bangs open the door.
So many wonders!
Life — the raw thing — sings and calls.

Cicadas clatter in wind-riffled grass.
Striped spinnakers race down the waves.

Heaps of wanton yellow leaves rustle and shake.
Fat, frantic squirrels shove nuts
into soft, forgetful earth.

Cold air pummels my lungs,
yanks my breath,
as crackling sunlight skims the frozen lake.

Snowdrop flowers stretch
and crest the porous snow.
Broken ice crashes into boulders
as swollen rivers pound the miles
towards ocean and home.

Forgetful, sloth-like by nature,
I rejoice in all these reminders —
to wake up, pay attention,
love relentlessly with my whole heart.

Summer's End

A breeze on evening's fringe
billows sheets on the line,
jostles the drooping magnolias
and singed grass.
The heat has dissolved.

You remember when you were young,
feeling the ache
as beach umbrellas closed,
and tourists, bags packed, scattered like leaves
past shuttered shops.

One more day, you begged,
to stretch awake under profligate sun,
air heavy like syrup from the scent
of honeysuckle, gardenia, jasmine.
For hardened bare feet
to kick up dust, burrow in wet sand.
To sit for one last night on the car's hood,
bare legs dangling,
and stare at the stars.

One more day before you returned
to school, schedules,
struggled to catch the bus, the subway,
the final bit of light
pulling you home.

You grieved, even as your mind
quickened in the fall wind.

Stroll backward to summer's beginning —
when time, unable to imagine freedom's end,
rolled down the hill into boundless blue.

Sitting on a Fence

"Why sit on a fence when you can paint it?"
Jimmy Moore, Radio KRUU.

I'll tell you why.

Because you can see
the white farmhouse and red barn,
the brown colt practicing
the bounce in his gait.

Because you can see both sides —
the field bereft of grass, bare to the wind,
and the field with five Herefords ruminating
on the lucky abundance of clover.

You can see, past the burned stubble of stalks,
a small constant stream
and dark loam ready for planting.

You can sit absolutely still
and not startle the young deer
at the edge of the trees.

Because, on occasion,
there is something better than doing,
under the bright and timeless sky.

V

Kaleidoscopic World

Field Guide to Curiosity

Once again, animal study has hijacked
our first-grade class.
"Teacher, why do you love animals so much?"
Derek sits with chin in hand,
stroking an imaginary beard.
Little man, wise already,
he strives to comprehend.

I love animals passionately.
Some I may never see,
certainly will never touch —
whales, sea horses,
rhinos, leopards, tarantulas, hawks.
All things that slink, slither, soar, swim.
That live without filter
their purposeful lives,
procreate, perish.

I yearn to crawl inside their skins,
to behold with my own composite eyes
their kaleidoscopic world.
My muscles twitch to invade their limbs,
to apprehend, almost from birth,
how to embrace a branch,
balance and perch.
How to sip nectar
and re-curl my hair-like tongue.
How to sit still for hours,
observe a small breath, strike,
savor the crunch of skeleton.

Derek patiently waits.
What he's asking but doesn't yet fathom —
Why human hearts expand
beyond craving and clutching.

I choose words his years can grasp.
"Because they're so different from us.
They're so interesting."

One day he will know in his bones
we are all bits of stardust,
yearning for connection
in the swirling arms of galaxies.

Monet's Water Lilies

"It took me a while to understand my water lilies."
— Claude Monet

With no idea how he was teasing Fate,
Monet dug his pond,
planted willows, added water lilies.
Every day, he walked along the shore,
but brought no brush or palette.

Then one day—the shifting beauty,
the tussle of flowing water,
floating flowers,
haunting purple depths.
The reflections of dripping branches
that wavered up toward the sky.
The frenzy of sparkle and shadow
changing every moment.

He began to paint fiercely,
absorbing color and light,
splashing and dabbing
the vibrating canvases.

How his water lilies made him suffer,
or so he claims.
Thirty years.
When he wiped his brushes and palette clean,
two hundred paintings shimmered on studio walls.

In the museum, reverent crowds
stand entranced.
Imagination wanders the curved path
at pond's edge,
while across the cool ripples,
light dances and laughs.

Wild Welcome

After reading "Little Horse" by W.S. Merwin

Welcome to the wild, Little Horse,
to our forest of pathless trees,
waterfalls, treacherous slopes.
You will find no safety here,
familiar as you are
with farm, stable, and stall.
No water trough or feedbag of oats.
No warm, pungent blanket
ready for your back.

You will soak in storm, freeze in snow,
blister in summer.
No one brushes your coat
or offers an apple.
Stumble on a root,
and your flesh will feed
a family of red fox.

But everywhere you turn your unhaltered head,
sun flickers among leaves,
races over waving grass.
Shade wanders through branches
cloaked in moss.
Endless rivers careen off boulders,
splash banks of willows,
carve out green canyons
that whistle in the wind.

You will never drowse
through days of sameness here.
And you can never be lost,
where everywhere is home.

Magpie

In Monet's miraculous canvas,
a magpie sits on a fence
in early morning snow.
Brilliant brushstrokes extend an invitation
to walk along the path that leads to the gate
and leave the first footfalls after predawn storm.
Blinding light and long shadows vie for the heart.

Yet the painting poses a riddle.
Bare branches can't feed this bird,
so why does the magpie sing?

In a humble building in the background
someone still lies in bed,
surfacing from eiderdown
with the sun's first smile.

Someone ready to stretch and rise,
    sweep snow from the stoop,
        and spread birdseed for the day.

Spring Vanishings

Salamander

Red pot turned upright.
Small dark flash,
writhing body startles back
into dark crevice—
his world.

Three Crows

Sick crow, eyes shut,
cowers behind the planter.
Two caws warn against desecration,
four glinting eyes guard
the sanctity of final breath.
By morning all has vanished.

Pine Cone

Pine cone bursts in rowdy wind.
Chipped, frayed,
death rattle,
seed world.

Ladybugs

In November, bushes sag.
From afar—masses of orange berries.
Up close—thousands of ladybugs.
A single pulsing organism
prepares to sleep.

In March, sun clears dense trees,
temperature climbs.
Soft breeze inhales,
then downbeat of baton
and bushes shake loose their burden.
Orange cloud rises, swells, exhales
into the emerald land.

Volunteer

Our Pittosporum tree shimmies in the breeze.
Thin pointed leaves with crinkled edges
and yellow central veins
hide clusters of green seeds.
The dense canopy shades families
of bluebells and forget-me-nots.

This 30-foot tree grew from a seed
some animal dropped
in a willing backyard corner.
We didn't know what it was.
Haphazard gardeners, we ignored it for two years
while it thrived in its private compact
with soil, sun, and intermittent rain.
The arborist finally told us,
"It's a Pittosporum. It must like it here.
They don't often volunteer."

We have watched it waltz in full sail
on windy nights, satin skirt rustling.
We've sat dry in its circle as steady rain
drizzled from its rim.
Each spring and fall, tiny white flowers
release a powerful perfume
that blesses the neighborhood.

Water's Edge

Whitecaps race to shore,
break, die, revive
in the brilliant bay.
White sails race the horizon's mist.
Blue spinnakers unfurl at the turn
and charge the red bridge.

At water's edge, a small boy
twirls and dangles
from his mother's hand,
a blue-clad gingko leaf.
Levitated in her arms,
he squirms and squeals,
furious to reclaim his exploits
in the swirling sand.

A red-tailed hawk, wind marauder,
scans the marsh for rustling gray.
Wings balance, tip
in the sky's scales,
then plummet into raw reeds.

Marsh rosemary shakes, tumbles,
and spills its riches
as insistent wind shoves me
down the path's rocky curl.

I had craved a contemplative walk.
Instead — a deluge of joy
as the sensate world engulfs me
in a full tide of rowdy gifts.

Cello Suite

This cello sings like a diva
full-throated, smooth.
Shining body, mahogany red,
responds to gentle hand.

That one, mellower, chestnut brown,
builds to the harmony,
vibrates with each bow slide
and haunts with sweet echoes.

And this one,
slight wolf in the bass,
sasses back,
winks in the filtered light.
An earthy French Cab,
proud of its 1910 provenance
and multitude of past lovers.

Enthralled, I listen
as chords spill out,
each cello its own personality.
Judging merits, critiquing faults,
even though I've never played a note.

Your mother loved music,
chose your first cello
when you were 10,
advised you on your second at 12,
knowing a cello would resonate
with your deep, pensive heart.
Now, at 65, in the wake of her departure,
you pluck and bow new cellos,
testing complexity, balance, tone.

I recall decades ago,
a bright Albany Christmas.
Snow sparkles in moonlight
as your cello reflects hearth light.
You pause, draw your bow and play.
Your mother, long skirt flowing,
glides sure fingers over harp strings.
As the warm air vibrates,
music enfolds us in velvet flames.

November Apples, Hudson Valley

The red barn and orchards shelter
beneath the Helderberg mountains.
Changeable weather and mottled sky
predict a midnight frost.

Traveling families swarm the small store,
an interminable line for cinnamon-dusted donuts.
Young children cluster round two young goats,
pat them, pull back,
as the goats lick and chew.

We have come to pay homage to your parents.
Every Albany autumn, your family drove
winding roads through brilliant colors.
You and your brothers spilled
from the station wagon, scattering ducks
as you ran whooping up the slope.
In their turn, our sons,
sparked by the sharp mountain air,
kicked crackling leaves
in their race to the stand.

One last time, I slip into the shed
crammed with bushels of ripe apples —
McIntosh, Red Delicious, Empire,
Jonagold, Cortland, Gala —
names that evoke centuries
of firm bright skin, crisp flesh.
Dozens of different scents tossed in air
mingle, begin the splendid descent
into fermentation and decay.

Mesmerized, I slowly spin,
seized by memory.
Perfect in this moment.
Pick it, eat it now!

After a Long Journey

After a long journey, the one we all know —
train wheels churning endlessly,
descending bottomless chasms,
clattering through smoke-filled tunnels —
the light is a surprise,
distantly remembered.
The soft lemon glow like a hand
gently stroking our clutched hands,
a finger tracing a worry line,
reminding us to smile.

Something shifts.
We remember now — we meant
to rise and stroll the birch forest.
Silver limbs bereft of leaves,
but clutching secret buds.

Blue Arc

Across the sky's holy blue arc,
brushed white clouds fade
to mare's tail whispers.

Cows drowse in the sere yellow fields,
swishing flies with lazy tails.
The dray horse's moist lips linger
over fresh-pitched hay.

Lying beneath this breath-filled expanse,
arms spread, palms up,
my body flattens,
so thin it could sigh
through a window crack.

I could dream for centuries,
and wake to a different world,
heart no longer yoked
to the steel plow.

Old Plum

Last night a wild wind
raged for hours,
yanked branches off our trees —
eucalyptus, mimosa, cedar and pine —
and tossed them across the yard.

It flayed the neighbor's plum tree.
Old, dry, gnarled.
"It was dying," he said.
"We talked about taking it down, but —"
he shrugged. "The wind got there first."

For hours he and friends cut limbs
and chopped at the trunk.
At day's end,
piles of firewood and mulch.

What survives pruning is stronger, leaner.
Ready for the next storm.
What lies on the ground —
a gift to the soil
to replenish what still stands.

When I am too old to bend,
may a gale take me down like that,
in a glory of shaking.

Rivers of Light

A gompa is a Buddhist shrine room.

Outside the gompa, the wind rises.
Bare branches whip in lightning and hail.
Sheets of rain saturate dry grass,
turn paving stones to ponds,
purify the muggy, pollen-soaked air.
We splash through the dark
as the bell rings.

On such a wild night,
Milarepa danced
in the drumbeat of stars.

Inside, women young and old
chant a three-part mantra,
voices resonating from ancient beams.
Rivers of light cascade from candles,
as songs of pure joy
flood the shrine.

Kayak at Twilight

Kayaking on the bay,
I meander through marsh
as day shortens and fades.
Silently, I dip my paddle into water,
push back,
and strike a trail of light.
A goddess creating her own path of stars
in indigo and silk.

In the distance, bay merges
with undulating ocean
and horizon dissolves.

Alone on the water,
alone in the world.

One day, I will slip
into the ebb current,
internal tide converging
with the world's great waters.

For now, I paddle in reach of shore.
A woman in love with stillness,
liquid starlight,
the smell of the sea
and salt-drenched song.

About the Author

MJ Moore has lived in Miami, Atlanta, Boston, and now the San Francisco Bay Area. Her various incarnations have included technical writer, environmental activist, farm apprentice, teacher, poet, Buddhist practitioner, wife and mother. Her odd collection of skills includes milking goats, driving a tractor, editing books on meditation and library format integration, directing first-grade plays, and chanting mantras in Pali. As a bicoastal being, she thrives on salt air, wind and waves, but also loves mountains and deserts. Poetry is a source of vision and joy, a way to engage the inner life of the heart and celebrate beauty in the world.

mjmoorepoems@gmail.com

CPSIA information can be obtained
at www.ICGtesting.com
Printed in the USA
FSHW010857160121
77755FS